FIVE MINUTES L

The Centenary of the

Higham Ferrers, Rushden, Wellingborough

Branch Line

Rushden Historical Transport Society

©

Rushden Historical Transport Society

1993

ISBN 0-9522426-0-5

Designed, typeset, printed and bound by
Stanley L. Hunt (Printers) Ltd., Midland Road, Rushden

Contents

FOREWORD   6

by A. J. George
(local photographer), son of Mr. Fred George, who was Station Master at Irthlingborough Station from 1908 to 1924

1893-1922—MIDLAND RAILWAY   9

by Chris Moorman

1922-1948—LONDON MIDLAND SCOTTISH RAILWAY   22

by A. J. George

1948-1969—BRITISH RAILWAY   29

by A. J. George

1984—RUSHDEN HISTORICAL TRANSPORT SOCIETY   84

by Chris Moorman

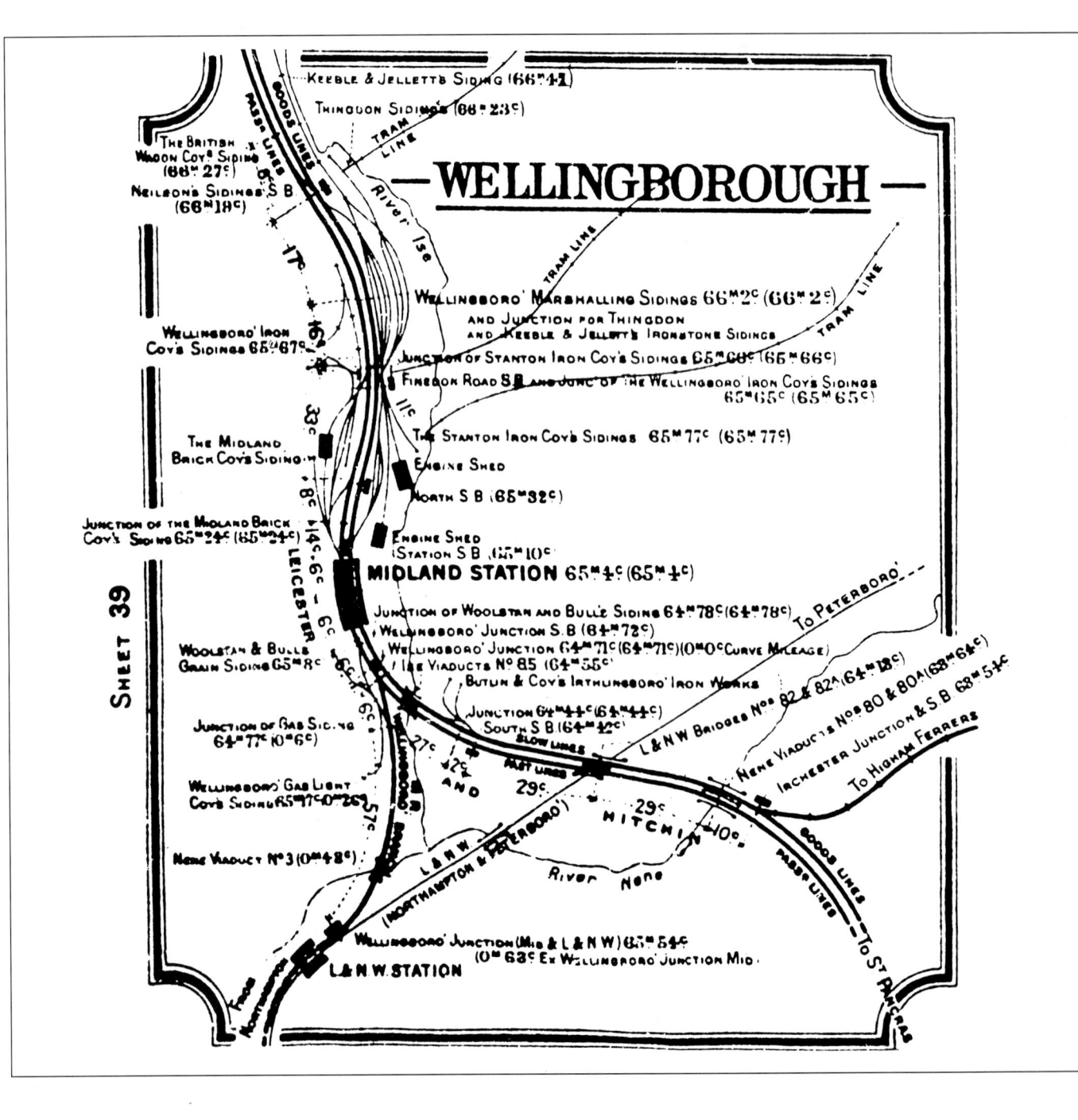

WELLINGBOROUGH

Sheet 39

- Keeble & Jellett's Siding (66m 41c)
- Thingdon Sidings (66m 23c)
- The British Wagon Coy's Siding (66m 27c)
- Neilson's Sidings S.B. (66m 18c)
- River Ise
- Tram Line
- Passr Lines / Goods Lines
- Wellingboro' Marshalling Sidings 66m 2c (66m 2c) and Junction for Thingdon and Keeble & Jellett's Ironstone Sidings
- Wellingboro' Iron Coy's Sidings 65m 67c
- Junction of Stanton Iron Coy's Sidings 65m 66c (65m 66c)
- Finedon Road S.B. and Junc of the Wellingboro' Iron Coy's Sidings 65m 65c (65m 65c)
- The Midland Brick Coy's Siding
- The Stanton Iron Coy's Sidings 65m 77c (65m 77c)
- Engine Shed
- North S.B. (65m 32c)
- Junction of the Midland Brick Coy's Siding 65m 24c (65m 24c)
- Engine Shed
- Station S.B. 65m 10c
- MIDLAND STATION 65m 1c (65m 1c)
- To Leicester
- Junction of Woolstan and Bull's Siding 64m 78c (64m 78c)
- Wellingboro' Junction S.B. (64m 72c)
- Wellingboro' Junction 64m 71c (64m 71c) (0m 0c Curve Mileage)
- Woolstan & Bull's Grain Siding 65m 8c
- Ise Viaducts No 85 (64m 55c)
- Butlin & Coy's Irthlingboro' Iron Works
- Junction 64m 44c (64m 44c)
- South S.B. (64m 42c)
- Junction of Gas Siding 64m 77c (0m 6c)
- L & NW Bridges Nos 82 & 82A (64m 12c)
- Nene Viaducts Nos 80 & 80A (63m 64c)
- Wellingboro' Gas Light Coy's Siding 65m 77c (0m 26c)
- Irchester Junction & S.B. 63m 57c
- To Peterboro'
- To Higham Ferrers
- Slow Lines / Fast Lines
- L & NW (Northampton & Peterboro')
- River Nene
- Nene Viaduct No 3 (0m 48c)
- Goods Lines / Passr Lines
- To St Pancras
- Wellingboro' Junction (Mid & L & NW) 65m 54c (0m 63c Ex Wellingboro' Junction Mid.)
- L & N.W. STATION

Colin Aitken – Chris Moorman – David Clipston
Co-Editors

1 Wellingborough Midland Road Station. Excavation and smelting of iron ores from local mines in the 1850's at Thomas Butlin's furnaces, were matched by the town's expansion from 5,000 to nearly 14,000 in the 1880's. Built in 1857 the station would eventually develop an extensive network of sidings, marshalling yards and engine sheds. This plan produced in 1914, shows some 17 sidings and three tram lines.
Courtesy Mr. D. Clipston

Acknowledgements

Great generosity has been shown and given by so many, whose contributions made the production of this book possible. Particular thanks are expressed to all who have loaned material included within the book, and assisted with necessary detail and information. Photographs are individually acknowledged throughout the book.

The intent of the book is to show 100 years of life around the railway and towns along the short stretch of line from Wellingborough to Rushden and Higham Ferrers. It is realised that much information comes from living memory, and the Editors accept that inaccuracies are bound to arise with copyright and acknowledgement, therefore no claims are made to be an authoritative history of the line, more than that indicated and gathered by the numerous contributors.

Keith Hill, Keith Hill Studios, for the Front Cover Oil Painting.

A. J. George, Photographer, for materials and specialist processes, and Foreword.

J. Whittington, Risdene Pharmacy, for Photowork donation.

J. & P & M. Osborne, Osbornes Sports and Toys, for guidance and donation.

Ms J. Etherton, Group Archivist, National Westminster Bank, London for photos and donation.

Fujicolour, for donation of film materials.

Evening Telegraph, for material and features.

Northampton Mercury for materials.

Radio Northampton, for broadcasting coverage.

KCBC Radio Kettering, for broadcasting coverage.

Northants County Council, for their wisdom and permission to use the site.

East Northants District Council, for their continued support.

RHTS, for all members who contributed information.

Foreword

As we celebrate the arrival of the railway at Rushden and Higham Ferrers, 100 years ago, let us consider did the railway bring prosperity, or did the rise in population and growth of the footwear trade bring the railway?

This is an Historical Transport Society, so let us take a dive back in history. The Romans came 1,950 years ago, stayed for 350 years, then told the Britons and Romano/Britons to look to their own defences. How were the Romans able to govern this remote extremity of their empire for so many years? They made straight paved roads and bridged rivers ignoring the contours of the land, this in a country of small almost self-sufficient settlements linked by bridle paths and rough tracks. On these roads legions boasted they could march 20 miles a day, followed by their supplies in horse drawn wagons.

The legions departed to defend Rome, their roads became overgrown, Villas and encampments became ruins. Viking raiders, Danish, Saxon and Norman invasions followed. Britons drifted back into the earlier ways of life, growth remained static.

The Black Death of the 1300's and the plague of 1665 each decimated the population by one in three or one in four.

From 1150 to 1380 the English Parliament was based in Northampton, the gentry concerned may have developed the first inklings of the footwear industry, requiring high quality footwear and good standard of boots for the army of those days. Over the centuries the footwear industry spread to other parts of the county.

Years past and roads were little more than farm tracks. In 1755 the local Turnpike and Toll Bar system generated funds to carry out maintenance, repairs and construction to improve travel by road, as horse drawn wagons were augmented by stage coach travel.

From 1808 to 1815 the Royal Mail Coach ran from London to Leeds Via Bedford, Rushden, Higham Ferrers and Melton Mowbray. At last services and goods were on the move. By 1800 the population of the Village of Rushden had outgrown the Market Borough of Higham Ferrers by nearly 100.

Waterway construction work began to harness water power with canals linking rivers. Peterborough was linked to Northampton via the River Nene about 1814, with local wharves at Higham Ferrers and St. Peter's Arms at Irthlingborough, before progressing onward to the Oxford Canal.

Staging posts for various stage coach operators existed at the Coach & Horses Inn at Rushden, the Green Dragon Inn at Higham Ferrers, the St. Peter's Arms and Bull Inn at 'Artleborough'. In 1831 a coach service to Buxton from London travelled this route, then on through Leicester and Derby.

There was a cross counties Stage Coach route from Buckingham to Cambridge, via Wellingborough and Thrapston. A dozen or more coaches each day carried travellers through Rushden and Higham Ferrers.

The London & North Western Railway 'Nene Valley' line opened in 1845 with a service from Northampton to Peterborough and stations at Ditchford and Irthlingborough. Within a few years the Midland Railway service from London St. Pancras to Derby was opened, with a station at Irchester.

Landowners in Higham Ferrers were unwilling to sell land for, or to build factories within the borough. This encouraged major building of housing and factories to take place in Rushden and Irthlingborough. Over a 10 year period the population grew in Rushden by 300, but Higham Ferrers by just 100.

The Rushden Gas Works opened in 1874, in a hive of small businesses behind the Lightstrung Cycle Works at the corner of Duck Street and Church Street. Higham Ferrers produced gas near the Walnut Tree. The lanes and farms such as 'Church Farm', at the junction of Church Street and Alfred Street in Rushden, became neat rows of Victorian terraced houses.

Large factories were built. John Cave's towering edifice on the High Street (rebuilt after the disastrous fire of 1877), were complimented by the impressive buildings of Jacques & Clark in 1890, at the juncture of Midland Road and Station Road, with the William Green Factory in Upper Queen Street, in 1895.

Commerce followed this brisk development. The National Westminster Bank (originally Northamptonshire Union Bank Ltd), was opened in 1889 and Lloyds Bank in 1893, along with a wide selection of shops on the High Street, to support growing demand and needs of the population.

The great opening day of the Midland Railway Station arrived 1st September 1893. The two gas companies united in 1891 to form the Rushden & Higham Ferrers Gas Co., and built new works in Shirley Road, Rushden, with a railway siding to take

6

wagons of coal from the new station. The story of the line could now be photographically recorded, as the following pages show.

By 1901 in just over 100 years, Rushden had grown from a rural Village of 818 souls, to a bustling, expanding and thriving Town of 12,450 inhabitants, adding 5,000 new townspeople between 1891 and 1901. Disaster struck in 1901 when the great fire at John Cave's High Street factory destroyed the building. By 1911 the population had increased by less than 1,000.

The First World War dominated lives between 1914 and 1918. At Higham Ferrers station a long platform of wooden railway sleepers was built near the A45, Kimbolton Road to accept *'Hospital Trains'* from France. The Parish rooms became a VAD Hospital staffed by local lady volunteer nurses. The platform was never used as intended, but the building was occupied by the convalescing wounded in their blue uniforms, awaiting discharge.

Rationing of foods and shortages of many essentials were endured during these four years.

The war ended with the railways in poor shape. Jobs had been promised to all who had served their country on their demobilisation. Other comrades used

2 Rushden's Northamptonshire Union Bank Limited (now National Westminster Bank), was purchased for £890 from a Mr. P. Hipwell. It was purpose built as a new banking office at a cost of £2,794 by Mr. J. Wingrove of Northampton and opened in 1889. First managed by Mr. J. W. Ashdowne until 1908.
Courtesy Ms. J. Etherton, National Westminster Bank Plc, Archives.

3 The staff of the Rushden Northamptonshire Union Bank c1924
Courtesy Ms. J. Etherton, National Westminster Bank Plc, Archives.

their discharge bounty to buy surplus 5 Ton Army lorries and started carrying and haulage businesses, serving local industry needs.

The railway companies would only carry the locally produced boots and shoes in sealed wooden cases, as they had to pass through so many hands. The new breed of carriers would accept small consignments of a half a dozen cardboard boxes of footwear, looped with string and deliver door-to-door, and at a considerably lower charge.

Omnibus services had opened new routes, but other ex-servicemen who bought T Model Ford and medium sized vans, fitted a few wooden seats, and competed for the trade, picking up passengers from the waiting bus queues in advance of the slow, solid-tyred motor buses.

Open *'Charabanc'* services with full loads booked in the towns, set off for outings and annual holidays at the seaside, competing with and taking a share of the railway passenger traffic.

4 Construction of the Wellingborough-Rushden-Higham Ferrers branch line, 1892. Viewed across what would soon become Rushden goods sidings. To the right of the picture and standing in front of the 'Eastfields' roofline appears to be a 'Manning-Wardle' contractors engine, from where factory workers are taking a lunch time break to view the progress of work. Note the 'American Steam Devils' excavating the 22′ 0″ of earth that required removal. It was purported that these machines would replace the labours of between 30 to 80 men. Originally a 'Stereoscope photograph' by Mr. S. Powell of Rushden.
Courtesy Mr. C. Wood

1893-1922 Midland Railway

The local newspaper the *Rushden Argus* on 9th October 1891 printed the following notice:

> MIDLAND RAILWAY – Mr. Ainsworth, an engineer of the Midland Railway Company, attended with plans of the new railway station, which showed it as situate in the field adjoining Mr. Mason's farmhouse. The station itself would be on the site of the footpath from the Backway to North-street, while it would be approached by a 25ft. road at an interval of about 12ft. beyond the line of the old houses. The plans, with the suggestion that a footpath should also be constructed (which was acceded to) were approved.

5 Higham Ferrers signboard c1893 originally sited on the wall of Ormes Factory on the approach to Higham Station, now carefully restored after missing from the county for many years.
Courtesy Mr. J. Osborne

6 Rushden West Groundframe c1893, originally sited at . . . Rushden Station. Carefully restored part of a large Midland Railway display.
Courtesy Mr. D. Harris

In December 1888 the branch line from Wellingborough to Higham Ferrers via Rushden was proposed, by local businessmen unhappy with the existing local rail transport links. The closest railheads were to the North at 'Irthlingborough' on the London & North Western Railway line from Northampton to Peterborough, or 'Irchester' to the West on the Midland Railway line.

The Midland Railway were asked to consider a loop line from Wellingborough, through Rushden and Higham Ferrers, to connect with the existing Kettering to Cambridge line at Raunds Station, some four miles further north.

Midland Railway replied that they would be prepared to recommend to their shareholders 'to promote a railway at the earliest opportunity', as they saw the potential for generating both passenger and goods traffic, from the steadily increasing boot and shoe industry in the region.

The Midland Railway's plans published in April 1889 were revised later that year to include a station at Higham Ferrers. These modified proposals were submitted to Parliament and the act received Royal Assent on 25th July 1890.

Construction of the line was not started until early 1892, under the general control of Walter Scott & Co. of Newcastle. The chief engineer for the line was A. E. Ainsworth. Mr. Parnell of Rugby was responsible for the erection of the station buildings at Rushden and Higham Ferrers.

The *Rushden Argus* on 12th August 1892 carried the report:

> THE NEW LINE – The Engineers report for the half-year says that the Irchester & Higham Ferrers branch is more than half done, and will be completed early next year. The expenditure for the half-year ending June has been for land £2000; for construction of line £10,156 2s 10d; and for law and Parliamentary charges £151 11s; making a total of expenditure for the six months ending June 30th 1892; of £13,047 3s 4d.

The line took approximately 18 months to build and an average of 400 workmen were employed. The line was only completed as far as Higham Ferrers as a local landowner refused to sell the required land, and, apparently built a row of cottages across the proposed path of the railway, to frustrate future progress,

The track layout at Higham Ferrers suggests that the Midland intended to complete the line to Raunds, since the running line was extended well beyond the run-round loop and goods shed connection, right up to Kimbolton Road.

As the line was now destined to be a short branch line, only one track was laid, although all the bridges and cuttings were constructed to allow a second track to be laid (presumably if negotiations to purchase that land, were successful!).

The great day arrived, 1st September 1893. The line was opened to goods traffic, bringing coal for local use.

The route was inspected by Major H. A. Yorke, RE of the Board of Trade on 9th March 1894 and approved for opening to passenger traffic, after two coupled engines made several runs over the road bridge near Rushden Station, to test for *'bridge deflection'*. Late alterations which had to be made at Wellingborough Midland Road Station costing £5,000 were carried out by E. Brown & Sons of Wellingborough to provide a covered footbridge and accommodation.

Passenger services commenced from Higham Ferrers on 1st May 1894, with crowds gathering at the station, bridges, embankments, even climbing trees to get a good view of the proceedings. Cheers greeted the arrival of the two Midland Railway trains, 0-6-0 No. 212 driven by Mr. Glover and 0-4-4 No. 2022 with Mr. Fred Seal at the controls. Station master Mr. A. Roper *'discharged his duties in a cool, calm and collected, yet diligent manner'*, as the train departed at 7.45 a.m. (five minutes late!!!).

7 Advertisements of 1892 that appeared in the 'Rushden Argus' newspaper, a fortnightly (free!) issue that also carried notices of the lines planning application and construction costs.
Courtesy Mr. C. Moorman

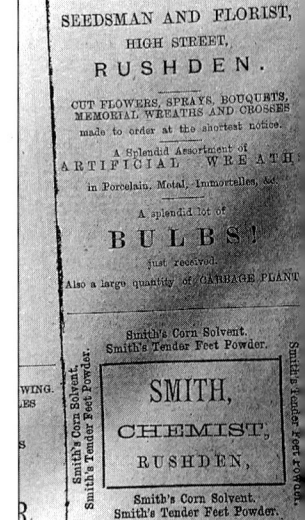

8 Advertisements of 1892 that appeared in the 'Rushden Argus' newspaper.
Courtesy Mr. C. Moorman

9 Advertisements of 1892 that appeared in the 'Rushden Argus' newspaper.
Courtesy Mr. C. Moorman

11 Advertisement of 1892 that appeared in the 'Rushden Argus' newspaper.
Courtesy Mr. C. Moorman

10 Advertisement of 1892 that appeared in the 'Rushden Argus' newspaper.
Courtesy Mr. C. Moorman

12 Poster advertising the opening of the new stations and goods services on 1st September 1893. *Courtesy Mr. P. Butler*

13 1894. View of Higham Ferrers Station, platform with dignitaries, prior to boarding the first passenger train to serve the line. *Courtesy RHTS Collection*

14 The opening day of passenger services 1st May 1894. Midland Railways 0-4-4 No. 2022 driven by Mr. Fred Seal pilots 0-6-0 No. 212 with Mr. Glover at the controls ready to pull 19 coaches. *Courtesy 'Evening Telegraph'*

The Rushden Argus
All aboard the branch line's first train

LAST week we told the story of the first passenger train to run on the Wellingborough—Higham Ferrers branch line sixty years ago. Now this rare photograph has come to light. It was lent to us by Mr. Reginald Cave, of Rushden—then the small boy seen halfway along the right-hand seat. In a saloon carriage of the first train are seen the dignitaries of Higham Ferrers, who were guests of the railway and evidently had a coach to themselves. The nearest figure on the left is Dr. John Crew. It has not been possible to identify all the others, but the Mayor of that time (Ald. W. Spong) and other members of the Corporation have been recognised. When the train stopped at Rushden the station approach was packed with high-spirited crowds and people clustered on every point of vantage near the track. The many passengers who joined the train at Rushden included members of the Local Board and other prominent townspeople. They moved off to a great burst of cheering, and on the train's arrival at Wellingborough an official reception was held. Mr. Henry Pitt was the Rushden stationmaster. He must have had a busy day, for the trains were packed with joy-riding crowds and excitement continued until a late hour. The fare from Rushden to Wellingborough was fourpence, and from Rushden to Higham one penny. Children could ride between Rushden and Higham for a halfpenny, and hundreds of them snapped up the chance to enjoy their first train ride.

15 Newspaper report of the opening of the line, showing the carriage interior, with civic dignitaries celebrating the start of a new era for services for the towns.
Courtesy 'Evening Telegraph'

16 1898. Wellingborough Train disaster. The Manchester express derailed to the North of Wellingborough Midland Road Station, by a luggage trolley which had fallen on to the line from the platform, resulting in a loss of 12 lives. Taken by Wellingborough photographer Mr. P. Brightwell on 2nd September. Note the Higham Ferrers train set in the foreground.
Courtesy Mr. J. Osborne

17 1898. Wellingborough Train disaster. The Manchester express derailed to the North of Wellingborough Midland Road Station. The steam crane is used to lift carriage sections from the trackbed. Taken by Wellingborough photographer Mr. P. Brightwell on 2nd September.
Courtesy Mr. J. Osborne

18 1898. Wellingborough Train disaster. The Manchester express derailed to the North of Wellingborough Midland Road Station. Crowds view the debris along the embankment. Taken by Wellingborough photographer Mr. P. Brightwell on 2nd September.
Courtesy Mr. J. Osborne

19 1898. Wellingborough Train disaster. The Manchester express derailed to the North of Wellingborough Midland Road Station. Upturned set of bogies lies next to this carriage from which the side has been torn out. Taken by Wellingborough photographer Mr. P. Brightwell on 2nd September.
Courtesy Mr. J. Osborne

20 Higham Ferrers Station staff of 14 persons, c1900. Note Bridge 13 in the background.
Courtesy Mr. C. Bryant

21 Timetable of the Midland Railways Wellingborough-Rushden-Higham Ferrers services, as published in the 'Rushden Echo' July 1901.
Courtesy Mr. C. Bryant

22 Engine Driver Mr. Short taken at Higham Ferrers Station c1901.
Courtesy Mr. R. Woodcock

23 An export order for footwear leaving John Cave's factory in College Street, Rushden, bound for Kansas City, USA 1910. Note the Midland Railway drays, and the goods packed in wooden crates. *Courtesy Rushden Rotary Book*

24 Midland Railways, Higham Ferrers ticket 1909. *Courtesy Mr. R. Woodcock*

19

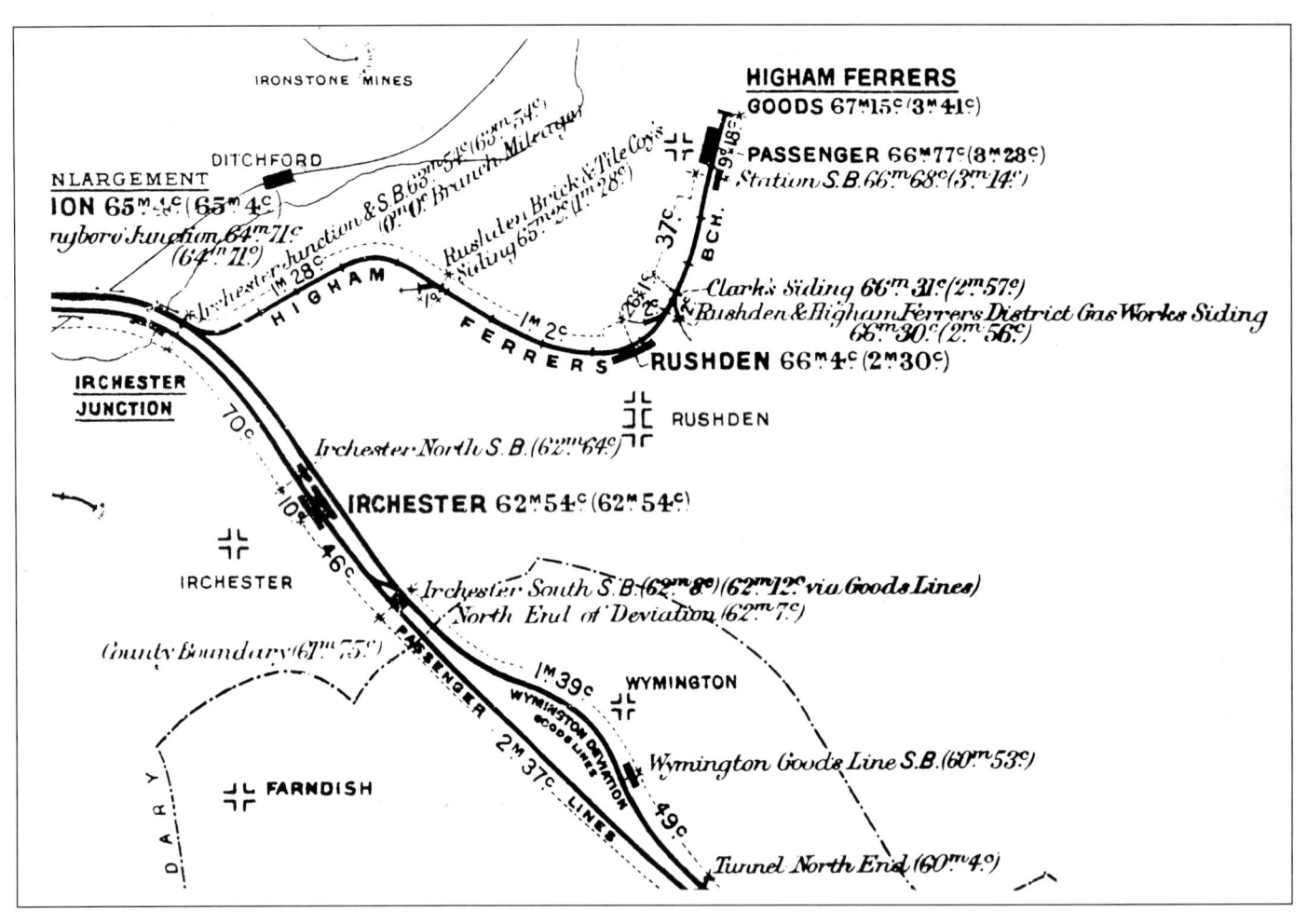

25 1913. Midland Railway line plan from Wellingborough, showing spur branch line via Irchester Junction to Rushden then Higham Ferrers.
Courtesy Mr. D. Clipston

26 1910. The Railway timetable for the Wellingborough-Higham Ferrers Branch line.
Courtesy Mr. D. Clipston

27 Mr. Mark Keep photographed at Higham Ferrers Station goods yard, with the dray horse c1913.
Courtesy Mr. R. Woodcock

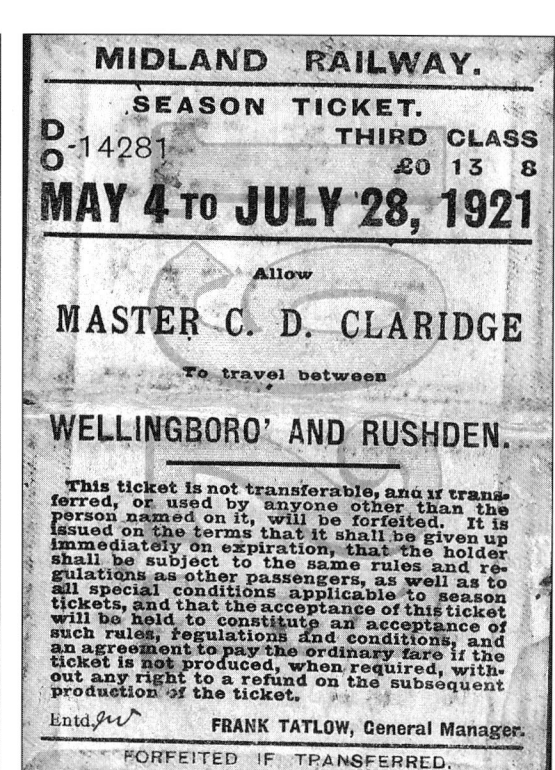

29 1921. Midland Railway Season Ticket issued to Master C. D. Claridge, son of J. Claridge (shoe manufacturer) on 4th May 1921.
Courtesy Mrs. R. M. Jenkinson

28 c1925. A motor vehicle of W. W. Chamberlain & Sons (manufacturers of 'Heel Stiffeners' for the footwear industry), alongside the LMS dray photographed at Higham Ferrers goods depot.
Courtesy Mr. J. Osborne

1922-1948 – London Midland Scottish Railway

Goods traffic was abundant and the early 1920's were quite prosperous as the economy surged forward. In earlier times The Midland and London and North Western Railway companies referred to each other as 'Foreign Lines', which changed as the merger of railway companies formed the London Midland & Scottish Railway. But the internal combustion engine was in ascendance. The railway companies with their old fashioned ways and poor management, were already on the decline.

Taking into account First World War casualties, the General Strike of 1926 and the depression extending from the mid-20's, the Rushden population in 1931 had grown by less than a 1,000 in 20 years.

Boot & Shoe and allied trades were also faced with short time working. Factories had failed to modernise. Some small firms who had started out with rented machinery had to close. A new entrepreneur named John White, investing in buildings, plant and machinery was able to succeed and grow.

The recovery from the depression had hardly begun, when War again broke out.

During the Second World War, Rushden endured three air raids. In the first raid, three bombs exploded near to the railway station. One landed in Shirley Road, breaking a gas main. One destroyed a portion of the right hand tower roof of the Queen Victoria Hotel. The other landed in Station Approach, all too close for comfort.

By 1940 many local men and women were away serving in the Army, Navy and RAF. With *'Allied'* forces many new visitors came to the towns, stationed at nearby Chelveston, Podington airfields and Knuston Hall.

At the time of Dunkirk the Canadians were the first arrivals. They were fast workers and married six local brides, although their stay with us was only about a week. The *'Hussars'* were here after Dunkirk, first issued with field guns and later with tanks. The Americans were 'all over the place', having bought up all the available bicycles.

30 The 'Waxey' (date unknown), at Wellingborough Midland Road Station, a twice daily service from Northampton to Higham Ferrers, so named because of the Waxes used in the local leather, shoe and footwear manufacturing industries.
Courtesy Mr. C. Bryant

For four years we suffered *'black out'* nights with heavy curtained windows, shields over car headlights, locomotive cabs shrouded with canvas hoods to contain the glow from an open fire-box door, dim hand lamps instead of platform lighting and drawn blinds in passenger trains to keep stray light at bay. A hand torch was essential if you walked at night, and batteries were scarce!

Footwear factories were *'Telescoped'* to make way for *'Shadow Factories'* to carry on, in case major war production plants were bombed out. There were 'Static water Tanks' to fight fires if water mains were fractured during air raids.

On VE Day an American Ordnance unit who re-treaded tyres at Birch's Garage hoisted the Union Jack and blew a siren until at last the steam ran out!

The war ended with the railway system worn out, services and supplies depleted, ration books still in use and the blizzard of 1947. Rushden was isolated by both rail and road for about three days. The call of the day was for 'Exports' to pay off war debts. Many servicemen after six years of military duties however were reluctant to return to their old jobs.

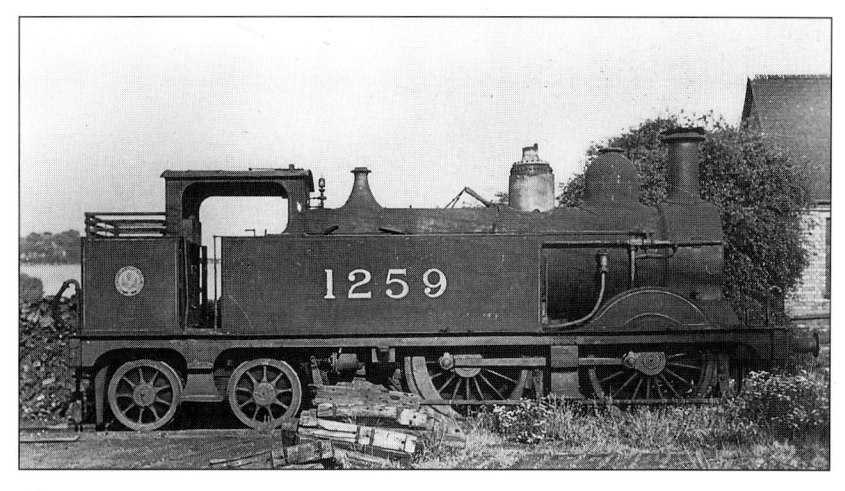

31 1934. LMS/MR Johnson 0-4-4T No. 1259 stored at Wellingborough Shed. Note the dome cover removed and placed atop the boiler. This locomotive was withdrawn later the same year.
Courtesy Ken Fairey Collection

32 c1932. Locomotive No. 1230 (Ex Somerset & Dorset Joint Railway 0-4-4T No. 52), at Higham Ferrers Station on 'Pulling' duty to Wellingborough Midland Road Station.
Courtesy Mr. R. Woodcock

Rushden Echo & Argus

When a lone raider swooped on a small Midland town on Thursday morning, one bomb wrecked a hotel, seen on the right, and damaged a cinema opposite.

Newspaper reproductions by courtesy of Mr. K. Garley and 'Evening Telegraph'

SCHOOL BOMBED IN MIDLANDS.

Lone Raider Swoops on Small Town.

DIRECT HIT ON FACTORY.

The fury and evil of war broke suddenly upon a small Midlands industrial town on Thursday morning, bringing the horror of Nazidom to workers and schoolchildren, and searing the streets with the dust and rubble of destruction.

FOUR ADULTS AND SIX CHILDREN (INCLUDING THREE EVACUEES) ARE REPORTED DEAD, AND SEVERAL PEOPLE SEVERELY INJURED, A NUMBER OF MINOR CASUALTIES ALSO RESULTING.

This town had been unvisited by the ravages of the war. It had begun the untroubled routine of another day. THOUSANDS OF WORKERS WERE IN THE FACTORIES; THE LOCAL AND EVACUEE CHILDREN WERE AT THEIR LESSONS IN SCHOOLS. Suddenly a lone plane wheeled across the sky, flying low across the centre of the town.

The plane dropped eighteen high explosive bombs and twelve incendiaries in a line across the town.

The air was split by hard, crackling explosions—one after another in a continuous salvo—and then the raider fled.

PEOPLE WERE DAZED.

For a few moments people everywhere stood dazed and unable to comprehend. Then, realising the truth, they ran from every quarter towards streets where destruction in those few moments had laid its deadly hand.

Right across the town the trail extended, beginning near the leading hotel and sweeping to a factory and school which stood on opposite sides of a short but wide and important street. There were direct hits on the factory and school.

For the FINEST COFFEE try—

JAMES BROS.

KENYA COFFEE ... 2/- lb.
ALBION BLEND ... 2/6 lb.
BLUE MOUNTAIN ... 3/- lb.
Freshly Ground for Each Customer.

Phone 2011 Wellingborough.

ALADDIN LAMPS
Instant Lighting. Silence in Operation.
ODOURLESS and SMOKELESS, SIMPLICITY and SAFETY.
Costing less than one farthing an hour to burn, and covered by guarantee of permanent satisfaction.
Cheapest method of modern lighting.

TABLE LAMPS, HANGING LAMPS
and all accessories in stock at

FAIREY BROS. 7, High St., RUSHDEN PHONE 308

Visit Our Showrooms—No Obligation to Purchase

FURNITURE
of every description. Quality and Price Right

J. S. TAYLOR, Ltd.,
(Opp. the Church) RUSHDEN. Phone 317.

SUMMERS & SONS, Ltd.,
15, 18, 18a, Midland Road, Wellingborough,

Baby Car Specialists,

Now Have a Good Selection of New Models in Stock.

Also Tan-Sad Folders, Nursery Furniture.

See Our Showrooms.   Phone 2771.

PRAED'S BITTER—

that's the stuff to give the troops.

33 Aerial view of Rushden Station (top right corner), 1923. The 'Station Approach' is a gated road, with no connection to Rectory Road as yet. Note the Queen Victoria hotel (Centre), alongside allotments (cultivated for over 60 years by Mr. Knight and his son Mr. Ken Knight), with Royal Theatre Cinema to the front. The railway stables are seen on the opposite side of the track, and more allotments where Mr. Cyril Freeman's Garage is to be built in the 1950's.
Courtesy 'Evening Telegraph'

34 c1943 The 'Tire Shop, Town Center, Rushden'. View North from near the railway bridge, towards Birch's Garage. The American Ordnance Depot, 305th Bombardment Group of the 8th Air Force, Chelveston took care of 'Camelback Ersatz rubber for tires' for AAF needs on fire equipment, dollys, jeeps, 4 x 4's, 2 ton trucks.
Courtesy Mr. G. Jones & Lt. Col. Stan Steffens USA (Ret) taken from 305th Bombardment Group (H) Memorial Association 'Can Do Notes' December 1981

35 c1943 at Wellingborough Station. American Air Force crew of the B17 bomber 'Half & Half' of the 305th Bombardment Group, 8th Air Force, taking time out from the Chelveston base. Left to right are Johnny O'Neill, Mel Meyer and Dick Neilsen.
Courtesy Mr. G. Jones & Lt. Col. Stan Steffens USA (Ret) taken from 305th Bombardment Group (H) Memorial Association 'Can Do Notes' December 1981

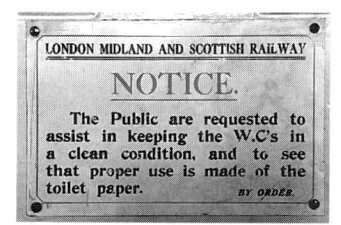

LONDON MIDLAND AND SCOTTISH RAILWAY
NOTICE.
The Public are requested to assist in keeping the W.C's in a clean condition, and to see that proper use is made of the toilet paper. BY ORDER.

36 Winter of 1947. Clearing snow from Rushden Station Goods Yard. Ration books, limited supplies and isolation by blizzard conditions for three days, still gave these men heart enough for a smile. The rumour that the person on the extreme left of the group is Mr. Richard Woodcock (founding member & chairman of RHTS), has been firmly denied.
Courtesy Mr. P. Murdin

37 1948. LMS Locomotive No. 8181 Class 8 Freight, at Rushden Station at the bridge, taken 8th May, ready for the John White's annual outing. Driver Wilf Boterill and Fireman Peter Bale of Wellingborough Motive Power Department (closed 28th September 1984).
Courtesy Mr. P. Bale

38 Mr. Ben Murdin, worker at Rushden Station, photographed at speed, going to work, during the summer of 1948.
Courtesy Mr. P. Murdin

1948-1969 – British Rail

Under a new national organisation the railway industry continued much as before. New steam locomotives designed and built at Crewe and Derby were introduced on Main line routes, with their elder (if less efficient), brethren serving and charming the growing number of photography enthusiasts on local lines.

New market materials such as bakelite, nylon and other plastics were to be seen replacing metal castings and fabrications. New product lines were introduced to take advantage of the 'new era' of man-made products. Less steel, coal and ironstone was required to be transported by rail.

In the early 60's the infamous Dr. Beeching was appointed head of British Rail and given the order *'Make the Railways Pay!'* Local ironstone mines were worked out, and cement production in the area had ceased, leading to the closure of the 'Nene Valley Line' in 1966.

The newly consolidated 'British Gas' had reduced demand for coal supplies, changing from 'town gas' production to the distribution of ready to use North Sea Gas. The foundries and steel producers enjoyed a temporary boom in business, with production of the huge steel pipelines needed for new gas supplies. The railway industry lost out on the transport of gascoal to the Gas Works.

Despite protests and petitions Rushden and Higham Ferrers stations closed on 13th June 1959 with the withdrawal of passenger services from the Wellingborough-Rushden-Higham Ferrers branch, apart from traditional August Bank Holiday excursions, which were retained until 1964. Crowds turned out to witness the passing of an era, many taking a final trip on the line, 3d return Higham Ferrers to Rushden. One or two took a memorial lump of coal!

Goods services still used the line. The circus with an elephant which was photographed about 1950 serves as a good reminder of the diverse range of 'goods' carried. Stage sets and scenery for the 'Ritz' Theatre productions were brought from West End Stages.

The closing act for scheduled goods services to

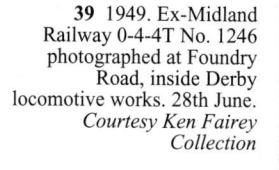

39 1949. Ex-Midland Railway 0-4-4T No. 1246 photographed at Foundry Road, inside Derby locomotive works. 28th June. *Courtesy Ken Fairey Collection*

29

Higham Ferrers came when the goods depot closed 3rd February 1969, and Rushden later in November 1969 with the closure of the coal depot.

Grass and bushes sprouted from the track beds after the rails had gone. Higham Station was demolished, and Rushden Station then unoccupied, deteriorated with the ravages of time and neglect. The Railway Bridge, a landmark of Rushden for so many years, had to go and was to me, the saddest sight of all.

The question asked at the beginning of the book, 'Did the railway bring prosperity to the two towns along the line? can be answered YES. It served the towns well as an artery, that brought in the life-blood of foods and perishables, and took out the goods produced locally, and it deserved a better fate.

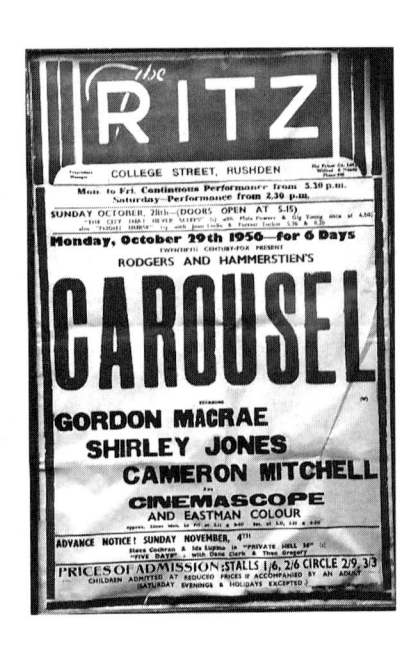

40 c1950's. The circus comes to town, and by train!
Pictured to the front and left of the elephant is Mr. Owen Newell who was a 'Shunter' at Rushden Station.
Courtesy of Mr. O. Newell

41 c1966 Rushden Station Goods Yard
Courtesy RHTS Collection

42 c1950's. John White's shoe factory outing to Brighton (close up).
Courtesy RHTS Collection

43 c1950. Ex-Midland Railway Johnson 0-4-4T No. 58053 approaching Irthlingborough Road bridge, Wellingborough, 'Pushing' with the Higham Ferrers 'Push-Pull' set on the 17th July.
Courtesy Mr. L. Hanson

44 c1953. DESTINATION TURKEY! Export order of Coal Washing Machinery manufactured by Covallen, Engineers of Rushden, seen to make a full train load as it departs from Higham Ferrers.
Courtesy Mr. A. J. George

45 1954. A standard school uniform of the day is worn by this young schoolboy, as Midland Railway 0-4-4T No. 58091 waits patiently on platform 5, at Wellingborough Midland Road Station with the Higham Ferrers branch train, on 2nd October.
Courtesy Mr. K. Fairey

46 1954. 'I want to be an engine driver when I grow up' or words similar to these perhaps were on the lips of this young admirer as he eagerly glances at the Ex-Midland Railway 0-4-4T No. 58091, as it pauses at Higham Ferrers Station with the branch train on 2nd October.
Courtesy Mr. K. Fairey

35

47 1955. Ex-London Midland & Scottish Railways 4F 0-6-0 Goods locomotive No. 44575 at platform 2, Wellingborough Midland Station, pressed into service on a summer excursion in the mid-50's. Note the use of the 'Blood & Custard livery' and the train indicator board, 'M' signifying that the train originated within the London Midland Region.
Courtesy Mr. K. Fairey

48 1956. Ex-Lancashire & Yorkshire Railway 2-4-2T No. 50650 prepares to form the next departure from Wellingborough Station, in early spring. Note the Engine men's hostel at top left, last used in the 50's and demolished around 20 years ago.
Courtesy Mr. K. Fairey

49 1956. Ex-Lancashire & Yorkshire Railway 2-4-2T No. 50650 pulls out of the carriage siding North of Wellingborough Station and runs into platform 5 with the Higham Ferrers train on 26th June.
Courtesy Mr. K. Fairey

50 1956. Ex-Lancashire & Yorkshire Railway 2-4-2T No. 50650 preparing to depart from platform 5 at Wellingborough Midland Road Station, with a train for Higham Ferrers, in early spring. Note extension of footbridge to platform 5, long since removed. Buffer stop of Northampton line bay platform 3, in foreground.
Courtesy Mr. K. Fairey

37

51 1956. Don't be misled by the milepost sign to the left of this Ex-Lancashire & Yorkshire Railway 2-4-2T No. 50650. The indicated 65 miles, is to London St. Pancras Station. The length of the Wellingborough-Higham Ferrers branch was $5^1/_2$ miles.
Courtesy Mr. K. Fairey

52 1956. Time for a breather on the platform at Higham Ferrers Station for engine driver Mr. W. Fairey, as Ex-Lancashire & Yorkshire Railway Class 2P 2-4-2T No. 50650 rests awhile, before returning to Wellingborough with the branch train, 6th August.
Courtesy Mr. K. Fairey

53 A rare sight to be seen on the Wellingborough-Higham Ferrers branch during 1956, was this Ex-Lancashire & Yorkshire Railway Class 2P, 2-4-2T No. 50650, photographed departing from Wellingborough Midland Road station, with the 'Push and Pull' set. The length of the Wellingborough-Higham Ferrers branch was 5¼ miles.
Courtesy Mr. K. Fairey

54 Midland Railway Class 3F 0-6-0 No. 43624 stands in the Higham Ferrers siding, at Wellingborough Midland Road station, with a short parcels train on 22nd August 1957. *Courtesy Mr. K. Fairey*

55 One other rare visitor to the branch was this Great Northern Railway 0-6-0 No. 64256. Seen returning to Wellingborough Midland Road from the Higham Ferrers branch hauling freight. The nearest locomotive depots to Wellingborough having an allocation of this class, were New England (Peterborough), and Hitchin.
Courtesy Mr. K. Fairey

56 An unusual visitor to the Higham Ferrers branch, during the summer of 1957, was this London Midland & Scottish railway 2-6-2T No. 40061, seen awaiting departure from Wellingborough Midland Road station, with the branch train.
Courtesy Mr. K. Fairey

57 1957. Ex-Midland Railways 3F 0-6-0 No. 43624 crosses from the slow to fast lines at Wellingborough Midland Road Station with a freight train from Higham Ferrers, on 26th September. This class of locomotive was originally introduced by Johnson in 1875 and rebuilt by Deeley and Foster from 1903 onwards.
Courtesy Mr. K. Fairey

58 1957. Ex-London Midland & Scottish Railway 4F 0-6-0 No. 44564, in poor condition, crosses from the slow to the fast lines on leaving Wellingborough Midland Road Station with a Higham Ferrers-Leicester train, on Boxing Day. The Higham Ferrers 'Push-Pull' set awaits its next duty in the background.
Courtesy Mr. K. Fairey

59 1958. Ex-London Midland & Scottish Railways Ivatt 2-6-2T No. 41328 draws forward into platform 5, at Wellingbrough Midland Road Station, with the Higham Ferrers train on 31st October. Mill Road Bridge in the background.
Courtesy Mr. K. Fairey

YOUR REF.		BRITISH TRANSPORT COMMISSION	OUR REF.	W.6.	B.R. 32602/2
DATED		**BRITISH RAILWAYS**	DATE	31.12.58.	

TO Fireman F. Farrington. 191.   FROM District MOTIVE POWER, Superintendent,
                                            Wellingborough. L.M. REGION

(Centre No.   )   Extn.........   (Centre No.   )

Loss of Uniform Cap.

Re the above, please inform me as to the place at which your cap was blown off, and whether you have made enquiries in that vicinity.

FOR H. H. BASFORD.

60 1958. This memo dated 31st December 1958, from the Superintendent H. H. Basford, Wellingborough Motive Power Dept, bids a happy new year to Fireman F. Farrington, in a very strange manner!
Courtesy RHTS Collection

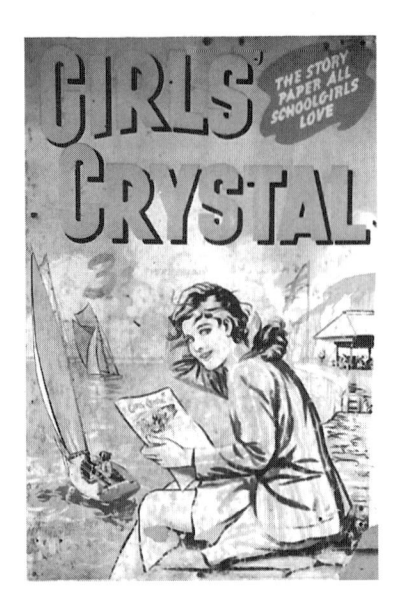

61 1959. Article in the 'Argus' 20th March. 'The girls of Rushden Secondary Modern Girls' School, waiting in 'crocodile fashion' for the train to Wellingborough to see the religious film 'Day of Triumph'.
Courtesy 'Evening Telegraph'

62 1959. British Railways 2-6-2T No. 41328 taken near Bridge 13, at Higham Ferrers Station.
Courtesy Mr. T. Heighton

63 1959. British Railways 2-6-2T No. 84007 alongside 42428 taken from the track bed by Bridge 13, at Higham Ferrers Station.
Courtesy Mr. T. Heighton

47

64 1959. British Railways 2-6-2T No. 41328 with an unusual angle on Higham Ferrers Station building.
Courtesy Mr. T. Heighton

65 1959. British Railways 2-6-2T No. 41328 taken from the track bed by Bridge 13 to the North of Higham Ferrers Station. *Courtesy Mr. T. Heighton*

66 1959. End of the run-round at Higham Ferrers Station, looking towards the goods shed.
Courtesy Mr. T. Heighton

67 1959. British Railways 2-6-2T No. 84007 at Higham Ferrers, 2-6-4T is seen in the 'run-round'.
Courtesy Mr. T. Heighton

68 1959. View taken from the train just south of Rushden Station. The Queen Victoria Hotel and Rushden Station can be seen in the distance.
Courtesy Mr. T. Heighton

69 1959. Goods shed to the North of Rushden Station. Note extensive use of goods yard.
Courtesy Mr. T. Heighton

51

70 1959. British Railways 2-6-2T No. 84006 stands in Higham Ferrers Station with the 'Push-Pull' set on 28th May. As can be seen this station is in immaculate condition, even in the twilight months of passenger service on the branch.
Courtesy Mr. K. Fairey

71 1959. British Railways 2-6-2T No. 84006 with 'Push-Pull' set awaits departure 28th May, from Wellingborough Midland Station en route to Higham Ferrers. The foreground shows the Wellingborough to Northampton line bay platform.
Courtesy Mr. K. Fairey

72 A general view of the Midland Railway Station at Higham Ferrers.
Courtesy Mr. K. Fairey

73 A general view of Rushden Station photographed from the approaching branch train on 28th May 1959. This was the only intermediate station on the Wellingborough - Higham Ferrers branch. Note the station barrow which suggests flourishing parcels traffic.
Courtesy Mr. K. Fairey

74 1959. 'Getting ready to catch it.' This is the scene at Irchester Junction signal box on 28th May. The fireman of British Railways 2-6-2T No. 84006 prepares to collect the single line working token from the signalman, prior to entering the branch line to Higham Ferrers.
Courtesy Mr. K. Fairey

75 1959. A very rare occurrence, seen in May, was the appearance of this Great Central Railway (a LNER rebuild), 2-8-0 No. 63742. Photographed on its return to Wellingborough Midland Road Station from the Higham Ferrers branch. Large numbers of these locomotives were to be found working the heavy industrial areas of South Yorkshire.
Courtesy Mr. K. Fairey

76 1959. Another view of the Great Central Railway (L.N.E.R. rebuild), 2-8-0 No. 63742. Photographed on its return from the Higham Ferrers branch to Wellingborough Midland Road Station.
Courtesy Mr. K. Fairey

77 13th June 1959. Business is booming as last day respects are being paid to the line. B.R. 2-6-2T No. 84007, 'sandwiched' between two sets of coaches, nears Irchester Junction with an afternoon train from Higham Ferrers to Wellingborough.
Courtesy Mr. K. Fairey

78 1959. London Midland & Scottish Railway 2-6-4T No. 42428 simmers in the Higham Ferrers siding at Wellingborough Midland Road Station, with a parcels train on 11th June. Note the Engine Men's Hostel top left.
Courtesy Mr. K. Fairey

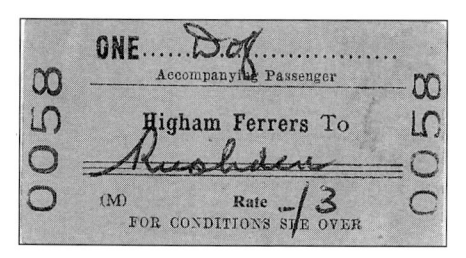

79 1959. The very last ticket to be issued at Higham Ferrers Station (note this passenger was a dog!).
Courtesy Mr. S. H. Elliot

80 1959. The last day of passenger services. Taken at Rushden Station on 13th June.
Courtesy Mr. L. Hanson

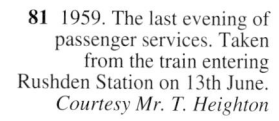

81 1959. The last evening of passenger services. Taken from the train entering Rushden Station on 13th June.
Courtesy Mr. T. Heighton

82 1959. Article taken from the 'Argus', Friday 3rd July of Rushden Carnival. The 'Float' shown carrying 'Closed' posters on the sign 'Rushden Station' did not worry these Strong and Fisher Ltd employees at Rushden Carnival. 'Rushden Undaunted' was their motto, and they brought out tricycle and pram for their transport.
Courtesy 'Evening Telegraph'

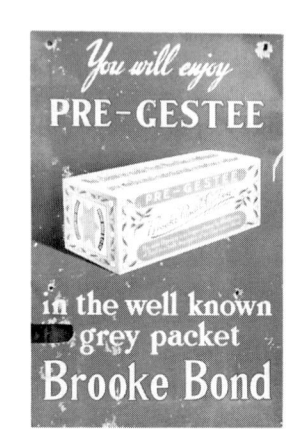

83 1959. British Railways 2-6-2T No. 84008 standing at Rushden Station.
Courtesy RHTS Collection

84 1959. British Railways 2-6-2T No. 84008, with a good view of the Goods shed to the North of Rushden Station.
Courtesy Mr. T. Heighton

63

85 1959. Ex-London & North Eastern Railways B1 4-6-0 No. 61381 with the return Higham Ferrers freight photographed at Irthlingborough Road, to the South of Wellingborough Station on 2nd June. The Nene viaduct can be seen to the right.
Courtesy Mr. K. Fairey

86 1959. Ex-London & North Eastern Railways B1 4-6-0 No. 61381. Higham Ferrers freight train photographed passing the Morris Motors foundry employing 800 workers (rebuilt in 1947-50). To the South of Wellingborough Midland Road Station on 2nd June.
Courtesy Mr. K. Fairey

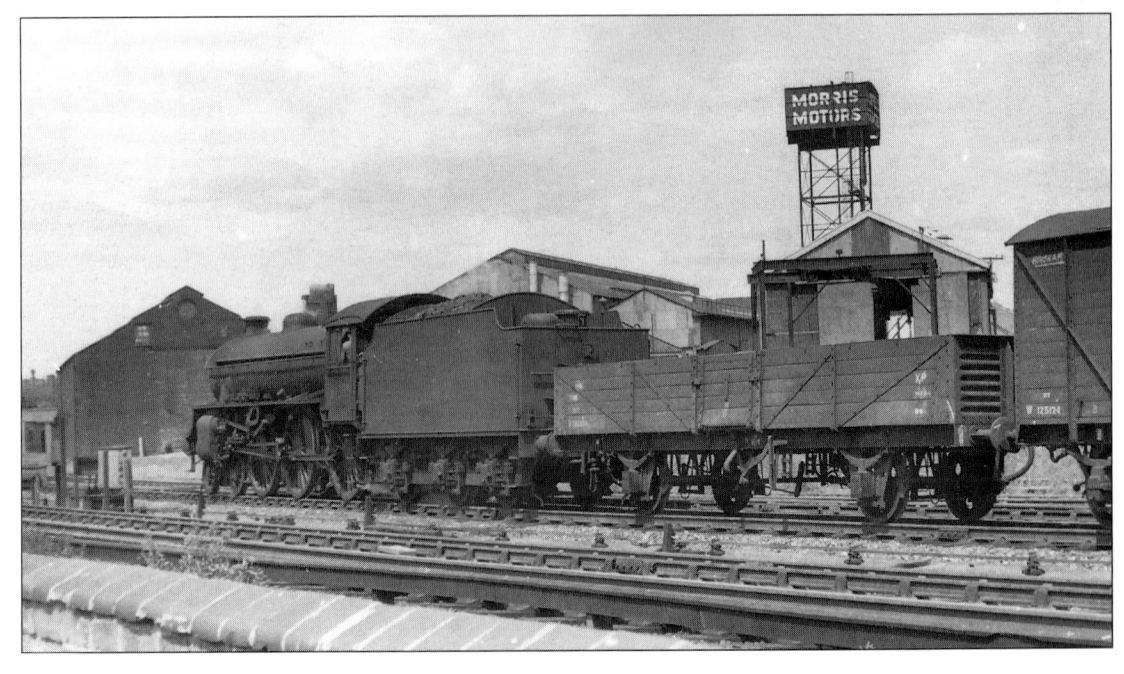

87 1959. Higham Ferrers set in platform 4 at Wellingborough Midland Road Station. Northampton train in bay at platform 3.
Courtesy Mr. T. Heighton

88 1959. British Railways 2-6-2T No. 84007 at Wellingborough Midland Road Station, platform 5. *Courtesy Mr. T. Heighton*

89 1959. British Railways 2-6-2T No. 84007 at Wellingborough Midland Road Station, platform 5. *Courtesy Mr. T. Heighton*

90 c1960. British Railways goods van at Rushden Station parcels office with (left to right), Sid Dungate driver, Mr. Abbott and Bryan Smith?
Courtesy Mr. C. Bryant

67

91 c1960. Entering the spirit for the 'Best Kept Station' award. Seen are Station master Mallone and . . . ?
Courtesy Mr. C. Bryant

92 c1960. Rushden Station Footbridge at night, in the snow. This enchanting view of an everyday object was made into greetings cards.
Courtesy Mr. C. Bryant

93 c1960. Rushden Station platform and canopy, entitled 'Busy Day'.
Courtesy Mr. C. Bryant

94 c1960. Old entrance to Rushden Brick Works, opposite St. Peters Avenue. The 'Electric Theatre' pay-office box is seen lying at a drunken angle at the foot of the embankment.
Courtesy Mr. C. Bryant

95 1960. London Midland & Scottish Railway Class 4F No. 44148 is seen with a short parcels train heading for Higham Ferrers along the (Up), slow line, running parallel to the Midland Railway line to London St. Pancras. Pictured just to the South of Wellingborough Midland Road Station, 8th September.
Courtesy Mr. K. Fairey

96 1963. The railway dray horse stables on the High Street in Rushden. Taken from Station Approach.
Courtesy Mr. C. Bryant

73

97 1964. Although the Wellingborough to Higham Ferrers branch line closed to passenger services in June 1959, the general goods and parcels traffic continued to use the line until 1969. Taken at Irchester Junction the London Midland & Scottish Railways 0-6-0 No. 44260 is seen having entered the branch line on 15th September. South Bedfordshire Locomotive Club organised a branch line 'Railtour', the train apparently called 'The Cobbler'.
Courtesy Mr. K. Fairey

98 1965. The Locomotive Club of Great Britain (Bedford Branch), organised this 'late day' brake van tour, over the Wellingborough-Higham Ferrers branch line. Shown arriving at Higham Ferrers Station on 3rd July, is British Railways 2-6-0 No. 78028. Note the platform is fenced off.
Courtesy Mr. K. Fairey

99 1965. The Locomotive Club of Great Britain (Bedford Branch), organised this 'late day' brake van tour, over the Wellingborough-Higham Ferrers branch line. Shown arriving at Rushden Station on the return journey from Higham Ferrers Station on 3rd July, is British Railways 2-6-0 No. 78028, with a view of the goods yard. Within 30 years this view is hardly recognisable.
Courtesy Mr. K. Fairey

100 The Locomotive Club of Great Britain (Bedford Branch), 'late day' brake van tour, over the Wellingborough - Higham Ferrers branch line. Shown entering the branch at Irchester Junction on 3rd July 1965 is B.R. 2-6-0 No. 78028. Note the splendid example of a Midland Railway semaphore signal.
Courtesy Mr. K. Fairey

101 1968. Diesel special, service No. B2, seen passing under the Rushden footbridge. The photographer's son, Mark, stands on the footbridge in May. Is this the last, last train on the line?
Courtesy Mr. E. Chamberlain

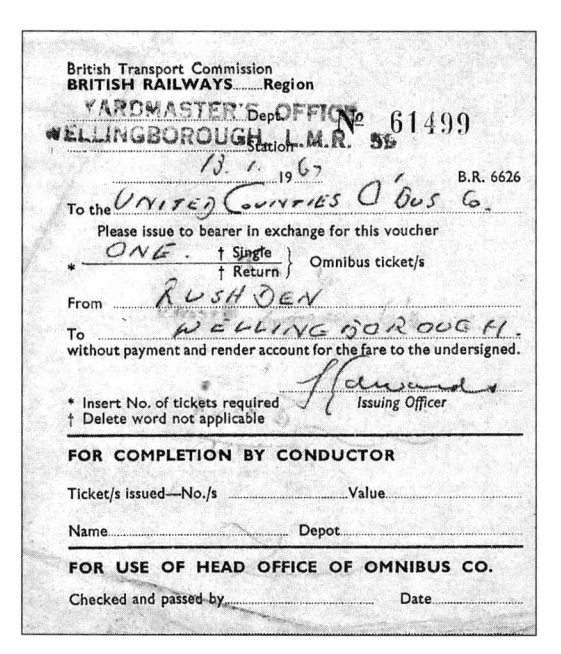

102 1967. A reminder of pre-1894 services. Before the opening of the Wellingborough-Higham Ferrers branch line, travellers used to commence their journeys by 'Omnibus' for transport to the main line station. This ticket No. 61499 issued at the Yard masters Office on 13th January permitted return travel by United Counties Omnibus Company, from Rushden to Wellingborough.
Courtesy Mr. D. Harris

103 1968. Looking from goods yard to Rushden Station.
Courtesy Mr. E. Chamberlain

104 c1970's. Disused station at Rushden, sports new sign, Blunsom Son & Co. Ltd., advertise 'DRIVE IN AND LOOK AROUND for Ladies & Gents Wear Household Drapery, Retailers for over 100 years.'
Courtesy Mr. C. Bryant

105 1973. Fateful days in March, when the dismantling of the Railway Bridge in Rushden signifies an end to an era. The scene of cutting the plates on the bridge is watched by a group of interested youngsters, and photographed by many onlookers.
Courtesy Mr. C. Bryant

106 1973. 'Vales of Northampton' removing a bridge section by crane.
Courtesy Mr. C. Bryant

107 c1975. View of the derelict Rushden Station and platform. The rails have gone and in their place grow scrub and bushes. Unkempt trees and overgrowth sprout from the platform and embankment.
Courtesy Mr. A. J. George

83

1984–
Rushden Historical Transport Society

The RHTS was founded in 1976, by a small group of people holding the informal, inaugural meeting at the Rose and Crown Public House, in Rushden. The title Rushden Historical Transport Society was adopted.

After two years of monthly meetings, trips and exhibitions it was suggested that a model exhibition be held in 1978 in the grounds of Hall Park, with just one or two cars! The Cavalcade was born, and has grown to become a major national event. The Society's collection of historic transport grew to include cars, lorries, buses and enamel signs.

In 1984 the opportunity to acquire a lease to occupy the derelict and dilapidated Rushden Railway Station was seized, with six members acting as financial guarantors to complete the legal documentation. The Society also obtained recognition as a Charitable Organisation.

The efforts of members, and voluntary services gradually brought the Station back to pristine condition. A short section of track was re-laid, and the site stocked with locomotives, carriage, freight wagons, steam crane and signal box.

A museum was created in the goods and parcels offices of the station, to which many members and visitors alike donated valued exhibits. A wide range of railway artifacts and memorabilia are kept on display. Attractive *'Ephemera'* and *'Street Jewellery'* adorn the building and the members' *'Victoriana Bar'*.

108 c1975. View of the derelict Rushden Station and platform. Windows are broken. Tiles are slipping off the roof. A sorry looking sight, awaiting re-birth. *Courtesy RHTS Collection*

Work and plans continued through the threat of demolition caused by a scheme to build an unwelcomed road through the site. Recent permission was granted to lower the footpath that crosses the track bed, to allow extensions for further rails to be laid. The station, sidings and Goods Shed buildings will continue to exist, for future generations to enjoy.

Popularity grows from listings in Tourist guides and visits made by holiday-makers, school parties on educational trips, and guests from overseas. In this centenary year the Society was proud to act as hosts for a district visit made by the twinning town of 'Lorelei' from Germany.

Future dreams include the re-erection of a footbridge over the line, development of the line northwards towards Higham Ferrers, use of the goods yard, and perhaps road bridges.

109 c1983. View of Rushden Station, Canopy and platform. A pioneering team of Rushden Historical Transport Society surveys the decay and dilapidations, the work will now be started.
Courtesy Mr. A. J. George

110 1988. Rushden Historical Transport Society's 10th Anniversary Cavalcade raises revenue to assist in the restoration of the Station, lay a short length of track, acquire a railway carriage and cell truck.
Courtesy RHTS Collection

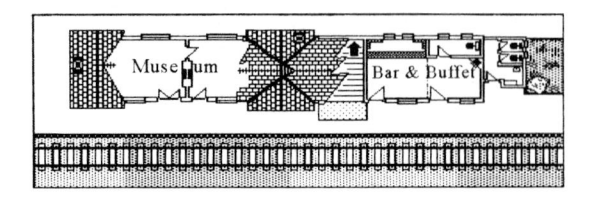

111 1990. An open day brings visitors onto the platform once again. New museum holds exhibits of railway and transport memorabilia, for future generations to enjoy.
Courtesy Northampton Mercury Co. Limited

112 c1991. 'I have seen the light' as the installed restored gas lighting at the head of Rushden Station entrance steps is lit, (by Richard Ashby) lending photographic charm to this picture and to the Machievellian clad figure disappearing into the brightly lit Station Buffet.
Courtesy 'Evening Telegraph'

113 1992. Refurbished, repaired, repointed, reglazed and repainted, Rushden Station looks resplendent with its fresh decor of 'Street Jewellery', ready to enjoy its second century of use.
Courtesy Mr. P. Barnes

114 1992. This 1954 British Railways Southern Region MK1 'tourist standard open' coach of the type made from 1951-63 that were built at Ashford in Kent and Eastleigh in Hants. It was originally numbered 3918, its early British Railways corporate 'Blood & Custard' livery was reinstated in 1992.
Courtesy RHTS Collection

115 c1991. An open weekend at Rushden Station, crowds thronging the platform, reliving a memory of a busy yester-year when people caught regular Trains from the platform. Shown is an 0-4-0 Ex-War Department diesel mechanical Loco WD48, built in 1942, acquired in 1988.
Courtesy RHTS Collection

116, 117 c1990. Memorabilia exhibits on display in the Station Museum, currently shows over 600 catalogued items, of working life around the railway.
Courtesy RHTS Collection and Mr. S. Brown

91

118 1992. Rushden Station platform and canopy restored to pristine condition shining in the brilliant summer sunshine. Note the reflection of the MK1 Carriage in the 'Waiting Room' window.
Courtesy RHTS Collection

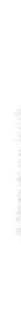

119 1992. Rushden Station 'Open Weekend'. Attracting crowds from far and wide. Centre of interest is the 'John Fowlers' steam traction engine 'Kingfisher'.
Courtesy RHTS Collection

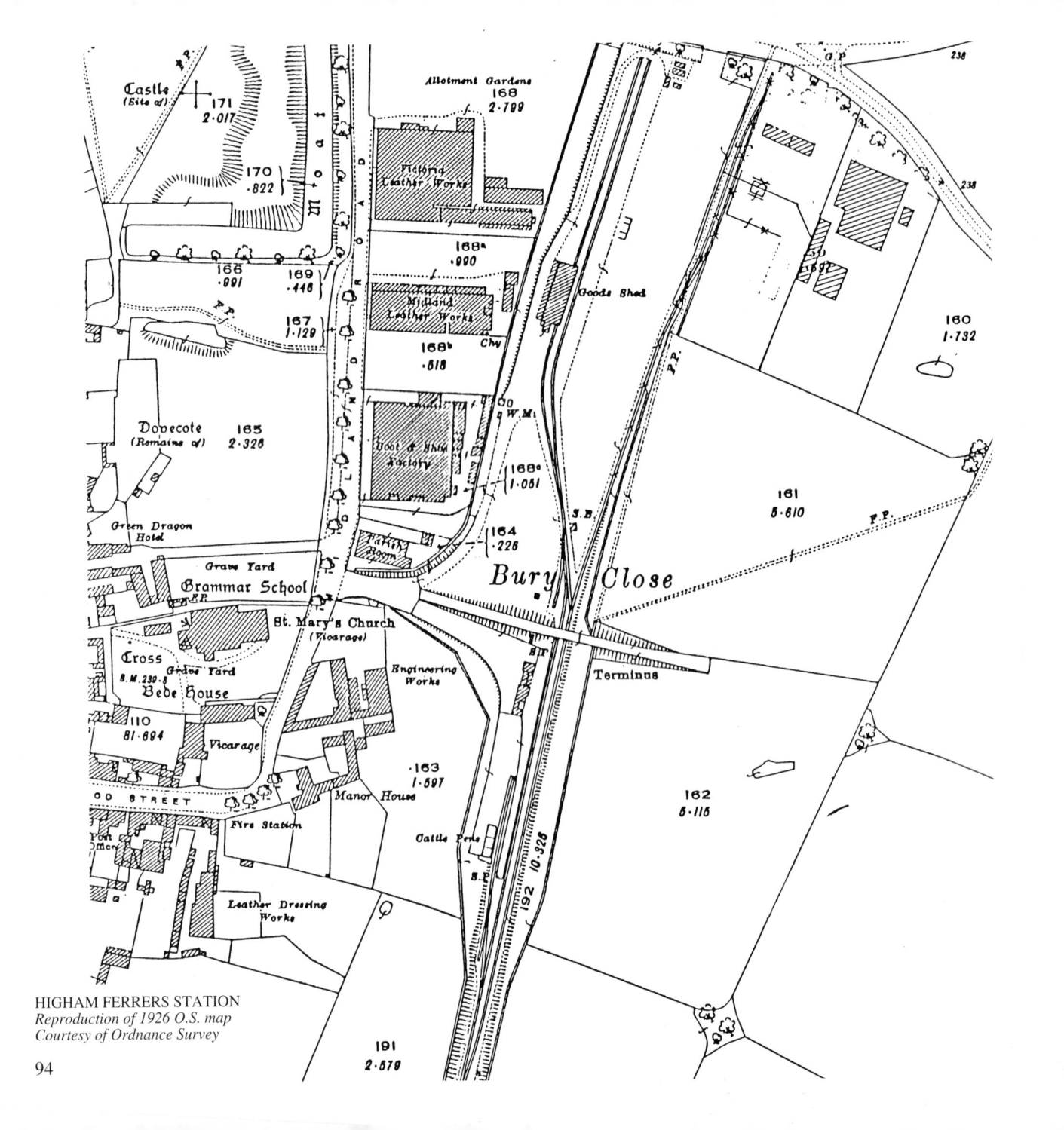

HIGHAM FERRERS STATION
Reproduction of 1926 O.S. map
Courtesy of Ordnance Survey

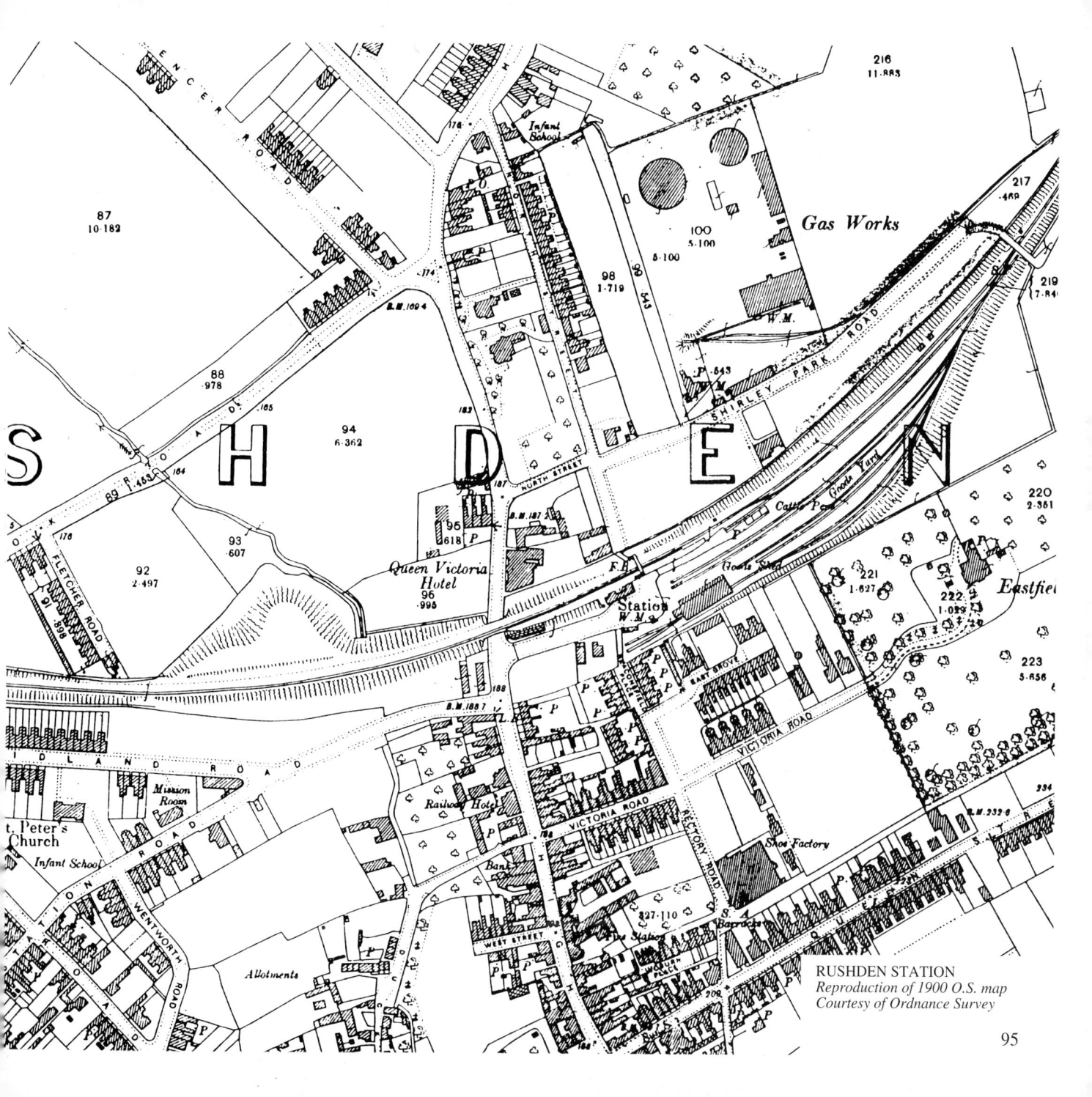

RUSHDEN STATION
Reproduction of 1900 O.S. map
Courtesy of Ordnance Survey

95

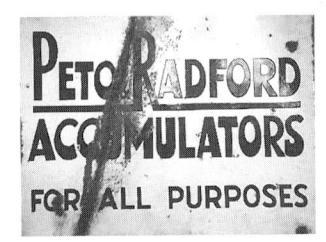

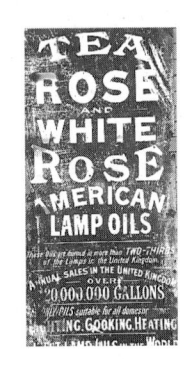

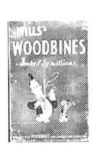

A selection of street jewellery from the past 100 years

96